Waterfalls
of
Grand Teton National Park

Charles Maynard

Photography By
David Morris and Janice Maynard

The Trails Illustrated Maps of Grand Teton National Park are some of the most accurate maps of the Teton's. They mark the falls that are listed in this book. The maps in this book are reprinted with the permission of Trails Illustrated. Maps can be ordered from:

Trails Illustrated
P.O. Box 3610
Evergreen, Colorado 80439

Published By Panther Press
P.O. Box 636
Seymour, Tennessee 37865

International Standard Book Number
1-887206-07-1

Waterfalls and cascades are beautiful but potentially dangerous. Please use every precaution and good judgement when visiting the park and its falls. Observe all posted warnings. The author and publisher are not responsible for injury, loss or damage incurred while using this guide.

FRONT COVER PHOTO:
BANNOCK FALLS BY DAVID MORRIS

BACK COVER PHOTO:
SPALDING FALLS BY DAVID MORRIS

CONTENTS

David Morris

GLACIER FALLS

Janice Maynard

A cascade below Taggart Lake with Grand Teton in the background

Teewinot

The central peaks of the Teton Range are called the Cathedral Group. They are rightly named, for they rival the spires of Notre Dame and Chartres. The Teton Mountains rise abruptly from the valley floor of Jackson Hole. They truly form a sacred, inspirational scene.

The first time I saw the snow-capped peaks, we stood at Togwotee Pass in a meadow of wildflowers. The Tetons, though distant, were enormous, breath-taking. It was difficult to believe these magnificent peaks were the Tetons of which I had read. No photograph had prepared me for their beauty.

Waterfalls are not the first thought that comes to mind when the Tetons are mentioned. Snow-capped rocky crags, sagebrush flats, a winding river, bugling elk, grazing moose, all are images of Grand Teton National Park. Waterfalls make up a lesser part of the landscape, but not a lesser part of the beauty.

Hidden Falls drops from Cascade Canyon toward Jenny Lake with a roar that drowns the chatter of the many people who have crossed on the ferry. Years ago, the first hike we made in Grand Teton National Park was to Hidden Falls. The power of the falls surprised those of us who were used to the less vigorous falls of the Smokies and other parks in the east. Here was a force to be reckoned with.

Winter in the Tetons locks the waterfalls and rivers in ice. The torrents are stilled for nearly six months. When the spring thaw comes in June, the falls swell to the finest shows of the year. This display is fleeting and soon passes as the snow melts into the dry months of summer and fall.

Water is a life-giving and formative force in Grand Teton. Trumpeter swans, as well as several species of ducks, moose and elk live in and around ponds formed by beaver dams. These animals depend upon the snows of winter to melt, cascade down the steep slopes of the Tetons, and be trapped by the work of beavers.

One day we decided to photograph the first light of day as it struck Grand Teton and raced to the valley floor. An added bonus was the full moon setting over Mount Wister only a half hour before sunrise. It was a wonderful display of shadow and light. After day had broken and the photographs were taken, we drove along the Moose-Wilson Road. Wildlife abounded in the cool of the morning. Elk fed on a hillside while moose grazed in the shallows of a pond. Ducks floated in the deeper waters of the same pond.

High above these creatures towered the massive Tetons, carved by ice and water. The U shaped valleys between the pinnacles were scraped out by glaciers from Ice Ages of the past. In the present, snow and water continue to sculpt the mountains and canyons.

One afternoon while floating down the Snake River, we saw an osprey dip and snatch a fish from the rippling waters nearby. The powerful bird rose into the blue sky with a wriggling trout in its talons. We continued our trip down the Snake to see otter frolicking along the shore, a blue heron patiently fishing in an eddy, and ducks paddling to get out of the way.

I admired our guide's ability to know which channel to take and to remember where wildlife lived. He pointed to a bald eagle in its nest high in a tree before we could actually see it. His experience in daily trips down the river opened our eyes to the wonders around us. My most cherished memory comes to me often in that moment between wakefulness and sleep. Once again I see the massive Tetons passing slowly by, serenaded by the sound of water flowing south.

David Morris

THE CATHEDRAL GROUP OF THE TETON RANGE.

Leonardo da Vinci said, "When you put your hand in a flowing stream, you touch the last that has gone before and the first of what is still to come." I gained a sense of this tie in the flow of water in the Tetons. Ice and water of past winters, past millennia, fashioned Teewinot, the place of many peaks. Water also holds what is to come. Water brings life and new shapes to the rocky summits.

Waterfalls are a part of this ongoing process of life and nature. The water cascades not only from the heightened peaks but from the snows of last winter. The waterfalls in Grand Teton National Park are spots to enjoy wildlife, the streams, the mountains, and life itself.

–CWM
1996

David Morris

BRADLEY AND TAGGART LAKES

Introduction

Teewinot - "many pinnacles" was the name the Shoshone used for the lofty jagged peaks of the Tetons. Later, French trappers called them Les Trois Tetons and the Three Paps. By whatever name, the towering summits and level valley floor are breath-taking. The Tetons offer spectacular scenery with numerous wildflowers in the summer and plenty of snow throughout the long winter.

Initial accounts of the Tetons came from fur trappers working in the Rocky Mountains in the early years of the nineteenth century. The stories were more about the bounty of beaver than the fantastic mountain scenery. It was the valleys or "holes" that interested the early trappers. The story of Grand Teton National Park begins far before any humans came to the area.

David Morris

JACKSON LAKE AND THE TETONS

GEOLOGY

The Tetons are among the youngest mountains in the United States, yet the rock that makes up the mountains is over 3.5 billion years old. Massive earthquakes along a 40 mile fault line sometime between 5 to 9 million years ago caused the western side of the fault to rise dramatically while the eastern side fell. The mountains were uplifted by these earthquakes while the valley floor dropped.

LEFT: THE DIABASE DYKE IN MIDDLE TETON

BELOW: THE GROS VENTRE SLIDE FROM JACKSON HOLE

David Morris

Janice Maynard

Today, six peaks soar above 12,000 feet, with Grand Teton over 13,700 feet. The entire displacement between the original plain which broke in two along the fault line is 25,000+ feet. This means that while the peaks are over one mile above the present valley floor, the corresponding material on the eastern side of the fault is four miles below the surface.

Sedimentary rock layers that covered the bedrock have been worn away to reveal the present gray stone. A small cap of sedimentary rock on the top of Mt. Moran is a remnant of the rock which has been eroded. In addition to the movement on the fault line, water has been a major formative force in the Teton range.

Liquid water cut V shaped valleys in the uplifted range. Later, in the Ice Age, frozen water in the form of glaciers ground U shaped canyons such as Cascade, Garnet and Leigh Canyons. Glaciers slowly moved down from the high peaks to the valley below, bringing rock. This glacier borne material built moraines at the mouths of the canyons. When the glaciers retreated, the moraines trapped water to form scenic lakes in the Tetons. Jackson, Leigh, Jenny, Taggart and Bradley are all present examples of these morainal lakes. The Pinedale Period of the Ice Age (25,000 years ago) had the most influence on the present day Teton country. The moraines which hold the lakes, the glacial till on the valley floor, and the U shaped canyons are all primarily from the Pinedale Period.

Gneiss and schist make up the primary rock types found in the Teton range. These metamorphic rocks were formed under high pressure far below the earth's surface. The light and dark bands of quartz in the gneiss are bent and twisted due to the pressure under which the stone was made. Schist is formed under the same intense pressures as the more prevalent gneiss. New minerals such as mica are grown during the formation of the rock. Schists usually split along the planes of the new minerals.

The Tetons are still being formed. The mountains continue to rise about one foot every 300 to 400 years. Water and glaciers also proceed to wear down the peaks. Two dozen glaciers can be found in the bounds of the park today. Five of these glaciers are on Mt. Moran alone.

Small, daily earthquakes are registered on seismic devices located at the Moose Visitor Center, which also has an informative exhibit on the geologic formation of the Tetons. On the eastern side of the park the Gros Ventre slide, which occurred in 1925, is an example that the landscape is still in flux.

The Snake River flows through Jackson Hole from Yellowstone National Park into Jackson Lake and then on to the south. Large terraces above the Snake River indicate that the river once carried much more water. Jackson Lake originally was formed by glacial action. A dam, completed in 1916, nearly doubled the surface area of the lake. The dam provides water for irrigation to Idaho farmers during the drier summer months.

The Teton Range is a wonderful textbook example of a block fault. The geological story of the region is readily apparent in the geography of the mountains and valley. Each waterfall is an illustration of the ongoing geologic processes which sculpt an area.

HUMAN HISTORY

As glaciers retreated 11,000 years ago, humans first came to the Teton region. The archeological evidence points to people who were hunters and gatherers. Most were not permanent residents of the mountains or valley but came seasonally in search of plants and animals. Possibly another motivation for early visits to the Tetons was religious. Stone circles, similar to others found in the West, silently greeted those explorers on the first recorded climbs of the Tetons.

In historical times many tribes of Native Americans came through the mountains to hunt in the valleys. The Shoshone,

Janice Maynard

CUNNINGHAM CABIN

Bannock, Blackfeet, Gros Ventre and others traveled through the Tetons while moving to hunting grounds. The harsh winters discouraged year round habitation. The Colter Bay Visitor Center houses a wonderful collection of Native American art and artifacts. This exhibit is a good window into the past lives of those who passed through the Tetons.

John Colter, a member of the Lewis and Clark Expedition, might have passed through Jackson Hole in the winter of 1807-1808 while searching for tribes who would trade at Manuel Lisa's fort on the Bighorn River. Evidence for Colter's visit is partial, so it is not certain he actually made it to the Tetons.

Soon after Colter's time, other trappers did come to the area. It is these early French trappers, who viewed the Tetons from the west in present day Idaho, that called the mountains Les Trois Tetons or The Three Breasts. Other trappers soon followed, mainly passing through the territory, rarely stopping.

Jim Bridger, Joe Meek, Jedediah Smith, Bill Sublette, Kit Carson, and David Jackson are some of the better known men who trapped in the Tetons. Many of these are remembered in the place names today, the most famous example being David Jackson for whom Jackson Hole and Jackson, Wyoming are named. The mountain men who participated in the Rocky Mountain fur trade later guided others into the area.

Jim Bridger scouted for the 1860 expedition led by Captain W.F. Raynolds. The 1872 exploration of Ferdinand V. Hayden was guided by Beaver Dick Leigh. It was on this trip that William H. Jackson, the photographer, and Thomas Moran, the painter, rendered some of the first pictures of the region.

The first permanent settlers arrived in 1884. A reminder of their life can be seen at the Cunningham Cabin which was constructed in the late 1880s. Other good depictions of early life in Jackson Hole can be found at Menors Ferry and Antelope Flats.

Ranchers and farmers were the original settlers of Jackson Hole. Dude ranching became another source of income in the early 1900s. The small communities of Jackson, Wilson, Moran, and Kelly all were established in the years around the turn of the century. Annually over 3 million visitors come to Grand Teton National Park to enjoy the beauty of the mountains.

A NATIONAL PARK

The first national park in the world was created in 1872 by an act of Congress which set aside 2.5 million acres in the Yellowstone area. The Teton range was not a part of this original district even though some felt it should have been. President Benjamin Harrison set aside a part of the Teton Range as the Yellowstone Park Timber Reserve in 1891.

The Teton Forest Reserve, which was created in 1897, included much of what is now Grand Teton National Park. In 1909, the Teton National Forest was formed out of parts of the

Yellowstone and Teton Forest Reserves. This national forest included most of the Teton range but not the valley floor.

The federal government made several moves to protect and preserve the natural resources of the Tetons. The establishment of the National Elk Refuge in 1912 was an attempt to care for the wintering grounds of the country's largest elk herd. The National Elk Reserve is on the northern boundary of the town of Jackson.

Horace Albright, a superintendent of Yellowstone during the 1920s, envisioned the addition of the Tetons to Yellowstone. He talked with residents of Jackson Hole about this concept. This idea was received with mixed but strong feelings. Some felt the government had too much control over land in the area, while others thought the scenic and natural resources should be preserved.

David Morris

COLTER BAY ON JACKSON LAKE

The story is told that Albright took John D. Rockefeller, Jr. on a picnic in the Tetons during Rockefeller's visit to Yellowstone in 1926. While on Lunch Tree Hill, near the present Jackson Lake Lodge, the two talked of a national park in the Tetons. Soon after, Rockefeller formed a company to buy up land in Jackson Hole for the purpose of donating it to the government for its inclusion in a national park.

Grand Teton National Park was established in 1929, but it did not include the valley floor of Jackson Hole. The park was made up of the Teton range and the glacial lakes at the base of the mountains. Local opposition contested the value of including Jackson Hole in a national park.

Bitter feelings on both sides of the argument caused rifts in old friendships in the area. President Franklin Roosevelt's proclamation forming the Jackson Hole National Monument delighted some and infuriated others. It was only in 1950 that the present boundaries of the park were drawn. The John D. Rockefeller, Jr. Memorial Parkway to the north, which is administered by Grand Teton National Park, commemorates Rockefeller's role in preserving the Tetons for all Americans.

Grand Teton National Park has over 330,000 acres with scenic lakes, peaks, and sage flats in addition to the wonderful peaks that the French trappers first called "Les Trois Tetons." Millions of people enjoy this special national park which has hosted presidents and peace talks, trappers and tourists, cowboys and dudes. Over 200 miles of trail traverse steep slopes and arid flats to take the visitor to wonderful waterfalls and scenic mountain vistas.

Raft trips on the Snake River are a wonderful way to see the mountains and experience the wonders of Grand Teton National Park. The sound of the water masks the approach of humans, thus allowing close encounters with much of the wildlife of the area.

MOOSE FREQUENT THE WILLOW FLATS IN THE PARK.

NATURAL HISTORY

Winter is the season that dominates over half of the year. The cold weather begins in what most of the country calls autumn and lasts well through late spring. Snow and ice lock precious life-sustaining moisture into glaciers and snow packs from the highest peak of Grand Teton to the valley floor of Jackson Hole. Yet even in the icy stranglehold of winter, life not only survives but thrives. Life most often flourishes near water.

Waterfalls provide a micro climate for life in the harsh macro climate of the Tetons. Water and food are more plentiful at the falls, the ponds, and the river. Wildlife, both plant and animal, tend to congregate around the water which Loren Eisley called "the miracle" of this earth.

The Snake River is crowded with life, from cutthroat trout to bald eagle to moose. The cutthroat trout, which gets its name from the red slash marking under the gills, is the only native trout in the Tetons. It is thought that the cutthroat originated on the Pacific coast. During the Ice Age the cutthroat migrated up the Columbia to the Snake. The trout then moved up the Snake River to its headwaters which include Two Ocean Creek. Volcanic activity and/or glacier movements changed the course of some of the streams to "trap" the cutthroat on the eastern side of the Continental Divide.

The Snake River cutthroat trout is a distinct cutthroat trout subspecies which is best identified by many dark spots on each side. Cutthroat trout travel upstream to tributaries to spawn in May and June when the river is swollen by the runoff from the spring melt. Other trout such as rainbow, brown and brook were introduced by humans for angling purposes.

Just as the fish feed on insects and plants in the river, other creatures feed on the trout. Eagle, osprey and otter all eat the many species of fish which thrive in the Snake. Other wildlife that live on the waters of the Tetons are trumpeter swans, sandhill cranes, and various species of ducks. These fowl feed in the shallows of the Snake River and in the many ponds of Jackson Hole.

One of the animals that attracted humans was the beaver. Fur trappers of the nineteenth century nearly trapped the beaver to extinction. Today many beaver live along the river and in small ponds of their own construction.

Moose graze on willows in the flats along the shores of the river or one of the many lakes in the area. These largest members of the deer family are often seen in the grassy spots under the cottonwood trees near the river. Other large animals found in Grand Teton National Park are bison and elk. A herd of bison lives in the park year round. DO NOT APPROACH these large creatures which need plenty of room.

Elk are abundant in Jackson Hole, especially during the fall and winter. Elk descend upon the National Elk Refuge for the long winters. The herd can number more than 15,000 in some years. Pronghorn antelope forage in the open sage flats, while mule deer stay in the forested areas.

In the higher country of the mountains many small mammals survive. The pika, yellow-bellied marmot, and golden-mantled ground squirrel thrive in the rocky terrain of the upper Tetons. Also abundant in the higher meadows are wildflowers of all types. The growing season is short, which only heightens the enjoyment of the floral display.

A float trip on the Snake River affords a relaxed view of much of the wildlife and scenery of the Tetons. Creatures and plants that crowd the river for life-giving water don't block the grander scenery of the Cathedral group in the not too distant background. A horseback ride or hike also offer ways to see and experience the richness of life in Grand Teton National Park.

WATERFALLS

Waterfalls depend on precipitation and temperature for water flow. Most precipitation is in the winter months, but comes in frozen forms. This means that the water that drops from the sky in winter doesn't drop over falls until later. Thus, winter may be the "wettest" while late spring has the greatest water flow.

Winter is the dominant season in the Tetons. Its icy grip extends from October through May. Numerous glaciers on the highest peaks never melt but glisten white even on the hottest days of summer. When the snows melt the creeks and river swell beyond their banks. The early French trappers called the Snake River "The Mad River" or "The Accursed Mad River."

In the melt-off days of May and June the waterfalls of the Tetons are at their best. Also, many creeks which have little water the rest of the year may display a beautiful falls in the spring.

Summer and autumn are the drier seasons with very little precipitation. To best observe waterfalls, precipitation and water flow must be considered. One problem is that when the water shows are the best, it is usually the most difficult to reach the falls. Stream crossing in high water can be dangerous or impossible. Always check stream and trail conditions before hiking into the backcountry.

It's important to follow all national park regulations while visiting the backcountry. Registration is required to enter the backcountry. Check with a ranger for the condition and status of any area. The National Park Service staff is more than willing to assist you in having a safe and enjoyable visit to the Tetons.

Grand Teton National Park has numerous cascades. This guide contains ten of the more accessible and interesting ones. It is by no means a comprehensive guide, but is intended to direct the waterfall aficionado or the casual visitor to places of beauty.

CLIMATE

The following charts will assist in understanding the flow of water in the Grand Tetons. Water flows the best in late May and early June when the melt of the previous winter's snow is at its height. The falls in the Tetons are overwhelming during this time.

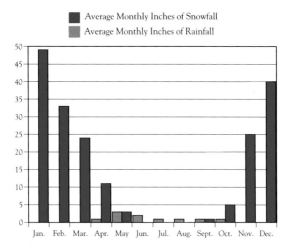

■ Average Monthly Inches of Snowfall
■ Average Monthly Inches of Rainfall

Average Monthly Waterflow on the Snake River

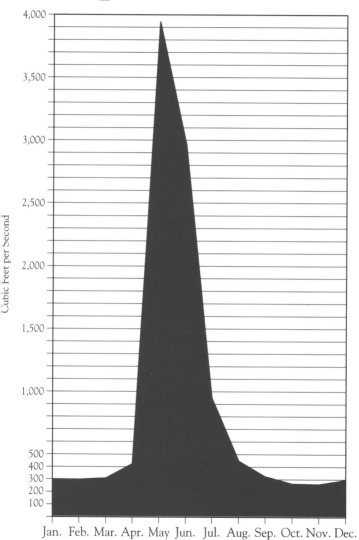

Cubic Feet per Second

4,000
3,500
3,000
2,500
2,000
1,500
1,000
500
400
300
200
100

Jan. Feb. Mar. Apr. May Jun. Jul. Aug. Sep. Oct. Nov. Dec.

David Morris

Hidden Falls

Waterfall Photography

Photographing waterfalls challenges photographers of all abilities. White water beside dark rock, harsh sunlight, green vegetation, and difficult terrain make that perfect photo elusive at best.

Composing that great picture can be tedious at times. Vegetation can obscure a waterfall to the point that a well composed shot is next to impossible. Debris can periodically clutter the base of the falls making the picture less pleasing. Try to shoot from different angles by standing in various places. Take time to study the picture in the viewfinder for composition.

Shutter speed is extremely important. Moving water is a pleasure to watch with the constant motion mesmerizing the viewer. Individual preference varies greatly on shutter speed and moving water. You must decide which is most desirable for you. A fast shutter speed will freeze the action to reveal individual drops and streams while slower speeds will blur the water. Since waterfalls differ considerably, study each one carefully. Some may elicit a feeling of power, others gentleness, still others grandeur. Each may indicate a specific shutter speed. It's best to shoot at several different speeds for each falls.

Here are a few suggestions to maximize your chances for getting that special waterfall photograph.

**Quality pictures can be taken with most modern cameras. Try a few shots with different lenses, if you have more than one. A telephoto lens can be useful in rugged terrain where a waterfall is difficult or hazardous to approach. A wide angle lens (24 mm to 35 mm) is nice for close shots which allow all of the falls to be included while eliminating unwanted surroundings.

**A sturdy tripod is a must for quality photographs of waterfalls, especially when using slower shutter speeds.

**Polarizing filters can be helpful in reducing glare from wet rocks on bright or sunny days.

**As a general rule, the slower films provide the best pictures of waterfalls. ISO 50 and 100 allow slow shutter speeds while giving nice color saturation. Since slower films have a finer grain, pictures or slides have a smoother texture and enlarge well.

**Waterfalls can best be photographed on overcast days that provide adequate but diffused light. On bright sunny days the best light will occur in the early morning or the late afternoon. It's helpful to know the orientation of a waterfall to the sun. For instance, if the sun rises over a particular waterfall, best results would be achieved in the afternoon with the sun on the face of the falls and the back of the photographer. Side lighting can be nice, but can cause harsh contrasting shadows.

**Metering a waterfall can be achieved in several ways. If possible, meter the white water, add one and a half to two stops, then recompose the picture and shoot. A similar result can be accomplished by metering on surrounding rocks or vegetation in the same light, recompose and take the picture as metered.

**Bracketing will usually assure a proper exposure. This is done by taking three exposures, one at the metered exposure, then one each at +1/2 and -1/2 stops. You will soon learn which exposure best suits your taste.

**Different shutter speeds will lend a varied texture to the moving water. The slower the shutter speed the more blurred or silky the water will appear. Try several shutter speeds to give you an idea of the different effect of each speed. Moving water starts to blur at about 1/15 of a second.

**Composing that special photograph can be challenging as well as fun. A tall, narrow falls usually looks best in a vertical format while a wide, short falls will look best in the horizontal format. With some waterfalls, it's difficult to know which will give the best results. In that case, take a few exposures in each to avoid disappointment. Take several pictures from as many angles around, above, and below the falls that caution and terrain will allow. From each position take several exposures at various settings and in the different formats.

The key to a good waterfall photograph is to take several exposures. Don't be afraid to make mistakes. Practice is the best way to learn. The more pictures taken, the better chance in having a good photograph.

The beauty of the Tetons' waterfalls is unique, but can be difficult to capture on film. With the exception of Hidden Falls, they generally have an easterly orientation, that is they face the morning light. Since early light is best for photography, this means rising early to start a hike or find a vantage point along a roadway.

Overcast days provide the best light for waterfalls photography but cloudless blue skies dominate the summer months in the Tetons. On sunny days, try to be in position to take the photograph you want by 10 AM. If you must shoot in the middle of the day, a polarizing filter can be helpful in reducing glare.

Several waterfalls in the Tetons can be seen and photographed from a distance. A telephoto lens is ideal for this situation. Keep in mind that the telephoto lens will not only bring the waterfalls closer, but will compress particles in the air and may give your photo a hazy look.

To photograph the accessible waterfalls in the higher elevations, I recommend getting on the trail at first light in order to arrive at the falls before the sun is too high. Unless you are planning an overnight trip into the backcountry I don't recommend late afternoon photos after the sun has dipped below the peaks. Late day sudden storms are extremely dangerous in the exposed terrain and hiking out several miles in the dark is hazardous.

Hidden Falls is difficult to photograph except on a nice overcast day. Tucked in a cove with lots of trees surrounding it, Hidden Falls is easily reached, but even the best morning light can cast harsh shadows. Since it is close to the boat dock, a late afternoon shot, with the sun below the horizon, may be your best option. Remember the overall light will be lower which means a slower shutter speed is required.

Like a person, each waterfall has a personality of its own. Whether at roadside or deep in the backcountry, each should be studied and listened to before trying to capture its beauty on film. Falls constantly change from hour to hour, day to day, season to season. Enjoy the hunt for the elusive, perfect waterfall shot.

—David Morris

About This Book

The visitor to Grand Teton National Park can easily miss the trees for the forest. The magnificence of the mountains is overwhelming. The waterfalls of the Tetons can be overshadowed by the massive snow-covered peaks. Many choices are available for touring this beautiful park. Every pulloff and trail has its own charm and advantage. The falls in this book have been arranged according to the watershed of the Snake River. Since water moves downhill, the text on each falls has been arranged as the river and tributaries flow. In the Tetons this is north to south. On each tributary the first falls is the highest one. The text follows the water down to the Snake. Thus Wilderness Falls is before Columbine and Spalding is before Cleft.

The size of a waterfall is difficult to determine. Where is the measurement to begin or end? When is a fall a cascade? Exactly where does a cascade begin or end? A cascade may be long without necessarily being very tall. What is to be measured? The cascade's height or length? For the most part the falls are measured according to their height, while the cascades are measured for length. Sometimes no accurate figures were available. The best estimate is often given.

Grand Teton is a park with several beautiful waterfalls. This book is only a partial guide to some of the better known and more accessible examples of the falls. It is not intended to be a comprehensive guide, but rather a beginning point for the waterfall enthusiast.

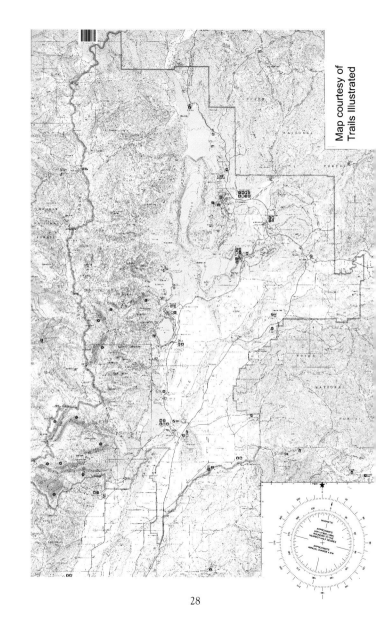

Map courtesy of
Trails Illustrated

Snake River

The Snake River, which begins in the southern part of Yellowstone National Park, is the largest tributary of the Columbia River. On its 1,040+ mile journey it passes through Wyoming, Idaho, Oregon and Washington. Its lamb-like beginning in Jackson Hole is nothing like its lion-like roar through Hells Canyon of Idaho where the river has cut the deepest gorge in the United States.

The Snake River has a character different from other rivers of the region. As a river, the Snake has no falls in the Grand Teton area. Its tributaries, however, are another story. Some spectacular displays drop from the steep slopes of the Tetons.

The sources of the Snake River are at the Continental Divide in and around Heart Lake which is at the eastern base of Mount Sheridan. The young river twists and turns through marshy areas to run south and west. At Yellowstone's South Entrance the Snake River, joined by the waters of the Lewis River, passes out of Yellowstone National Park into the John D. Rockefeller Memorial Parkway. The river flows southward to be lost for a while in the waters of Jackson Lake.

Although Jackson Lake was a natural lake formed by glacial action, a dam was built in 1916 nearly doubling the surface area of the original lake. The waters of the Snake River are controlled for irrigation purposes. The water is usually released in late summer for farmers in Idaho.

In Grand Teton National Park, the river's swift but gentle nature allows it to be used by rafters, canoers, and kayakers. Commercial rafting on the river has increased in past years so that many enjoy the Snake River from water level. The river's journey through the national park is marked by many shallow channels which twist and turn one upon the other like an unbraided rope.

Snake River near Flagg Ranch

The river is lined with aspen, cottonwood, sagebrush, and alder. Otter, beaver, eagle, and osprey live on or near the Snake. Moose, elk, bison, and deer populate the willow flats and open plains of Jackson Hole. The open nature of Jackson Hole doesn't make wildlife more abundant, simply more apparent.

The Snake River was not named for its serpentine track through the landscape nor for an abundance of reptiles. It was named for the Shoshone tribe which lived in the region. The name "Snake," referring to the Shoshone, was actually a misunderstanding. When asked their name, the Shoshone gave an undulating hand signal in reply. To the early whites it was thought to be a symbol for "Snake" instead of "Weaver" which is what the native Americans were actually signing.

William Clark named the river for his partner, Meriwether Lewis, in 1805. The name, Lewis River, had limited popularity, but wasn't used by the fur trappers who called it La Maudite Riviere Enragee or "The Accursed Mad River." The section of the Snake River in Grand Teton National Park is swift but not as mad as it becomes downstream.

The falls in Grand Teton National Park are on tributaries of the Snake River. The terrain of the Tetons is vastly different from that of Yellowstone. The steep mountains of gneiss and granite have no foothills but rise abruptly from the glacial plain of Jackson Hole. It's interesting to note that volcanic action formed most of Yellowstone, while plate tectonics and glacial action shaped the Tetons.

The Snake River is used by many people for different purposes. Although the water of the Snake River is stored for irrigation during the drier summer months, it is also preferred for recreational purposes. Fishing, rafting, canoeing, and kayaking are all popular ways to enjoy the river.

David Morris

WILDERNESS AND COLUMBINE FALLS

))) WILDERNESS FALLS
250+ Feet
Roadside Views

Wilderness Falls is an enormous falls which can be seen from many vantage points in Jackson Hole. It drops more than 250 feet over a cliff at an elevation of 9,200 feet. Waterfalls Canyon begins at Wilderness Falls as the creek rushes down to Jackson Lake.

Ranger Peak (11,385 feet) to the north, Doane Peak (11,355 feet) to the west, and Eagles Rest Peak (11,258 feet) to the south surround the beauty of Wilderness Falls. It's easy to lose the falls in the immensity of the mountain scenery. However, once it is spotted it is hard to miss thereafter.

A boat trip, a hike with no trail and a climb are required to reach this practically inaccessible falls. It can easily be seen from Lunch Tree Hill above Jackson Lake Lodge or from the Colter Bay Trail. From Lunch Tree Hill it is nearly seven miles to Wilderness Falls. The Colter Bay Guided Nature Trail brings you to within four and a half miles. Binoculars close the distance to allow good views of the water as it passes through a narrow opening to plunge to the rocks below.

Wilderness Falls begins its descent through a 6 foot wide crack on the cliff. This narrow chute holds the water for a quarter of its height. Then the water fans out into a wider falls. By the time the water strikes the base the falls is over 40 feet wide. The water on the rock behind the falls darkens the rock face to give a shadow-like appearance.

A 200mm or greater telephoto lens with a sturdy tripod allows good pictures on clear days. The falls face east, so morning light is the best. By mid-afternoon Wilderness Falls is in the shadow of the cliff.

))) COLUMBINE FALLS
200+ Feet
Roadside Views

Only 0.5 miles downstream from Wilderness Falls, Columbine Falls is a long curving cascade through Waterfalls Canyon. Columbine Falls, named for the beautiful wildflower growing in abundance there, is easy to spot. Wilderness Falls usually catches the eye first. Columbine Falls is below and to the north (right) of Wilderness Falls.

At 8,500 feet above sea level, Columbine Falls tumbles over rocks which have fallen from the cliffs above. The cascade begins in this stoney jumble with a 20 foot width. The water spreads to 35 feet and divides into several streams one third of the way down. The main flow of the creek runs to the south (left) while several smaller streams flow to the right. The entire creek reunites to form a flow of 45 feet in width.

Like its sibling falls, Columbine is difficult to reach but simple to see. It is easily observed from the road or a boat on Jackson Lake into which its waters flow.

))) RIBBON CASCADE
100+ Feet
Lake or Roadside Views

A small stream flows through Hanging Canyon between Symmetry Spire (10,560 feet) to the south and Mount St. John (11,430 feet) to the north. The stream begins from several glaciers to move into Ramshead Lake then Arrowhead Pool before it slides down the steep face of the Tetons to Jenny Lake. As it tumbles toward the blue waters of Jenny Lake, Ribbon Cascade is formed.

Ribbon Cascade is a long series of small falls and cascades which can be seen to the north of the boat dock on the western side of Jenny Lake. Though no marked trail ascends to Hanging Canyon (which "hangs" nearly 2,000 feet above Jenny Lake), it is possible to walk up to Ribbon Cascade. The best photographs are taken from the shuttle boat which regularly crosses Jenny Lake. From the vantage point of the boat the entire cascade can be seen.

Ribbon Cascade is particularly striking in June when the runoff from the winter's snow is the strongest. By late July the stream flow has dwindled, making the stream scarcely visible amid the rock and greenery on the mountain slopes.

HIKING TO RIBBON CASCADE: Begin at the West Shore Boat Dock on the trail to Hidden Lake. After 0.2 miles the String Lake Trail turns off to the north (right). Beginning at 0.5 miles from the dock, are four footbridges. After the fourth bridge an unmarked but clear trail follows the stream up to Hanging Canyon. At 7,800 feet, or 1,100 feet above the lake, Ribbon Cascade begins to splash down the mountain.

Janice Maynard

Hidden Falls

HIDDEN FALLS
200 Feet
1.2 Miles or 5.2 Miles Roundtrip

Hidden Falls is one of the most popular hiking destinations in Grand Teton National Park. The 200 foot cascade is a frothing show of force at the end of a scenic glacier carved canyon which is aptly named Cascade Canyon. Hidden Falls is actually a cascade and not a true falls.

The clear waters of Cascade Creek turn as white as the snow it once was as it pours over the jumble of banded gneiss. The snow-fed creek, swollen by the spring melt in June, roars over the rocks throwing off a fine mist. Englemann spruce, Douglas and subalpine fir surround the cascade. The stream begins small but widens considerably about one third of the way down. Hidden Falls faces south, so it is fully illuminated a good part of the day in the summer. Its bright white makes it difficult to photograph.

Located near one of the many fault lines that stretch across the face of the Tetons, Hidden Falls shares this same fault with Cleft Falls at the mouth of Garnet Canyon to the south. The name "Hidden" comes from the fact that it cannot be seen from the road through Jackson Hole as can most of the other falls in the Tetons. A hike is required to see the cascade in its grandeur.

HIKING TO HIDDEN FALLS: The easiest and most popular route to Hidden Falls begins at Jenny Lake. A shuttle boat crosses the lake in twenty minute intervals from 8 A.M. to 6 P.M. A modest fee is charged for the roundtrip ride. From the West Shore Boat Dock the trail goes to the south (left) and ascends through a spruce-fir forest. The trail crosses Cascade Creek once before reaching a spur trail at 0.5 mile. The short spur leads to a good view of Hidden Falls.

David Morris

Broken Falls

It is well worth the time and effort to walk on to Inspiration Point (only 0.5 mile further) and on up into Cascade Canyon. The scenery is stupendous. From Inspiration Point the views are of Jenny Lake, Jackson Hole, the Gros Ventre and Wind River Mountains. Also from Inspiration Point is a nice view of Cascade Creek winding its way to Jenny Lake below. The National Park Service has a small brochure "Cascade Canyon Trail" which highlights and explains many of the features on this walk.

200 yards beyond Inspiration Point, toward Cascade Canyon, cross the bare rock to the south (left) of the trail to look at the beginning of Hidden Falls. This short side excursion reveals the cascade above Hidden Falls where the creek turns from its easterly flow to move south.

An alternative route is on the Jenny Lake Trail around the lake instead of riding the shuttle boat. This adds 4 miles to the roundtrip. This route also begins at the Jenny Lake Ranger Station near the East Shore Dock. The trail follows the shore of Jenny Lake to meet the trail from the West Shore Boat Dock near Hidden Falls.

BROKEN FALLS
300+ Feet
Roadside - Near the beginning of the Lupine Meadow Road which is off Teton Park Road south of South Jenny Lake Junction.

Broken Falls is a long series of cascades which trip and turn down the steep, rocky face of the Tetons just below Teewinot (12,325 feet). Teewinot is the Shoshone word for "many pinnacles" and probably was applied to the entire range. The peak was named by Fritiof Fryxell, Grand Teton National Park's first naturalist, and by Phil Smith after they finished the first ascent of the jagged mountain in 1929.

David Morris

GLACIER FALLS

The stream flows across much bare rock, cascading and falling down the mountainside in a "broken" manner. Many small individual falls possess a beauty and charm of their own. Viewed as a whole, the cascade, which begins around the 8,300 foot mark, is a sight when it is swollen with the spring runoff in June. By July the flow begins to diminish. The show is pretty much over by August.

The water of this small unnamed stream tumbles over Broken Falls to flow into Moose Pond and a few smaller ponds. It then moves through Lupine Meadow into Cottonwood Creek, which also drains Jenny Lake, to go into the Snake River.

The best view of Broken Falls is from the Lupine Meadow Road after it turns off Teton Park Road south of South Jenny Lake Junction. Hiking to the side of Broken Falls requires much rock climbing beside the creek. This is not advised or necessary to view the entire cascade.

GLACIER FALLS
50 Feet

Roadside - Lupine Meadow Parking Area at the end of the Lupine Meadow Road off Teton Park Road south of South Jenny Lake Junction.

Glacier Creek flows out of Teton Glacier (10,100 feet) down into Delta Lake. A little before reaching the flat plain of Jackson Hole, Glacier Creek drops over a ledge in a two step falls.
Banded gneiss can be seen under the water and at the stream's edge. The water strikes a shelf one third of the way down, then flows over the shelf to form the second part of the falls.

Glacier Falls is along one of the many fault lines that cross the Tetons. It is the same fault line on which Bannock Falls to the southwest is formed. The Tetons are a result of drop fault action along a major fault line to the east of this smaller fault. Waterfalls

Spalding Falls

are often found on fault lines because the mountain is "broken" or faulted on that line.

Unlike Broken Falls, Glacier Falls is fed by the runoff from a glacier, in addition to melted snow. This means there is a steady flow throughout the summer months. It is more forceful in the spring when it is reinforced by the winter's melting snow.

The water of the creek has a milky appearance. This is due to the fine powder, sometimes called glacial flour, which is made as stone is ground by the glacier high on the mountain tops. As a rule of thumb, clear water means snow runoff, while milky water indicates glacial action.

The falls is west of the Lupine Meadow Parking Area which is at the end of Lupine Meadow Road south of Jenny Lake. The parking lot can be crowded as several popular trails begin there.

SPALDING FALLS
100+ Feet
10 Miles Roundtrip

Spalding Falls is a long cascade in the high Tetons at the head of Garnet Canyon. Runoff from Middle Teton Glacier forms a silver boomerang-shaped cascade over bare rock. A few Douglas and subalpine fir near Spalding Falls are the only trees in Garnet Canyon. At 10,000 feet above sea level, Spalding Falls is the highest of Grand Teton National Park's named falls.

Bishop Franklin S. Spalding, for whom the falls is named, was a member of the first recognized ascent of Grand Teton in 1898. Spalding, W.O. Owen, John Shive, and Frank Peterson passed near the falls on their historic ascent. At present, the most popular climber's route to Grand Teton passes to the east (right) of the falls.

The water remains in a narrow (4 to 5 feet) stream in the descent over the banded gneiss. The stone drenched by the stream is darker than the surrounding stone of Garnet Canyon. The canyon, carved by glaciers, was named for the presence of garnets in the rock.

Another interesting geological feature of the area is the diabase dike bisecting Middle Teton. A distinctive black line rises out of the canyon's floor toward the summit of Middle Teton (12,804 feet). The dike, twenty to thirty feet wide, was formed when molten magma pushed into a crack in the Precambrian rock. Another large dike can be seen near the peak of Mt. Moran.

HIKING TO SPALDING FALLS: The strenuous hike to Spalding Falls begins at the Lupine Meadow Parking Area which is at the end of a spur road off Teton Park Road 7.5 miles north of Moose Junction and just south of South Jenny Lake Junction. The small unpaved spur road leads 1.7 miles to the parking area.

Begin on the Amphitheater/Surprise Lake Trail to climb 700 feet in the first 1.7 miles to a trail junction. Continue on straight past the Valley Trail to climb another 900 feet in 1.3 miles over 5 switchbacks through beautiful alpine meadows to another trail junction. At the fifth switchback, the Garnet Canyon Trail branches off to the southwest (left).

The views from the Garnet Canyon Trail are breathtaking. Jackson Hole, Bradley and Taggart Lakes, and the Gros Ventre Mountains are only a few of the sights in the distance beyond the wildflower covered meadows. The trail is less steep from the trail junction into Garnet Canyon. After one mile the trail ends in a boulder field. To venture further requires registration at the Jenny Lake Ranger Station for off trail hiking. Registration is an important safety precaution for even the most experienced hikers and climbers.

Continue 0.5 miles through the boulders to reach a scenic meadow. Walk carefully on the climber's path to a good vantage point from which Grand Teton, Middle Teton, and Spalding Falls can be seen. Snow can block the way on this hike until the beginning of July. Check at the Jenny Lake Ranger Station for trail conditions. This is a strenuous walk, but is most rewarding.

David Morris

CLEFT FALLS

CLEFT FALLS
50 Feet
8 Miles roundtrip

The water from Middle Teton Glacier, which has already dropped over Spalding Falls and through Garnet Canyon, cascades again at Cleft Falls. Hidden among wildflowers, subalpine and Douglas firs, Cleft Falls is at the base of Garnet Canyon (8,600 feet). From the bottom of the falls the terrain drops steeply toward Bradley Lake far below. The stream flows through a "cleft" in enormous boulders just below a small pool.

One of the many fault lines which runs north to south is under Cleft Falls. This fault has caused a greater drop in the canyon floor at this point. The fault line at Cleft Falls is the same one shared by Shoshoko Falls to the south and Hidden Falls to the north.

A series of small cascades below the "cleft" makes the entire Cleft Falls a scenic spot. The trees cast shadows even in midday, making photography difficult. Early morning might be the best time to seek that perfect picture of Cleft Falls since the falls face east.

HIKING TO CLEFT FALLS: The strenuous hike to Cleft Falls begins at the Lupine Meadow Parking Area which is at the end of a spur road off Teton Park Road 7.5 miles north of Moose Junction and south of South Jenny Lake Junction. The small unpaved spur road leads 1.7 miles to the parking area.

Begin on the Amphitheater/Surprise Lake Trail to climb 700 feet in the first 1.7 miles to a trail junction. Continue on straight past the Valley Trail to climb another 900 feet in 1.3 miles over five switchbacks through beautiful alpine meadows to another trail junction. At the fifth switchback, the Garnet Canyon Trail branches off to the southwest (left).

David Morris

BANNOCK FALLS

Walk 0.75 miles to an open area with the creek far below. Garnet Canyon is ahead with Middle Teton at a distance. Drop off the trail through a rock field to move down toward the creek. Remember that ANY off trail hiking requires registration at the Jenny Lake Ranger Station. It is important that ALL off trail ventures be registered.

It is easiest to hike to the stream below the falls then move upstream. The large boulders at the "cleft" prevent safe hiking downstream. It's a struggle to reach Cleft Falls, but it's a nice secluded spot. (The first part of this hike is the same as that to Spalding Falls.)

BANNOCK FALLS
200+ Feet
6 Miles Roundtrip

The stream from Middle Teton Glacier passes over Spalding Falls, through barren Garnet Canyon, over Cleft Falls where trees and wildflowers dot the area, to flow over the long Bannock Falls in a lush green area. Mosses, ferns, shrubs, wildflowers, and subalpine fir crowd the banks of the stream as the water slides first down a long chute then spreads out into a wider cascade.

Bannock Falls is named for the Bannock tribe which lived west of the Rockies in the nineteenth century. The Bannock hunted bison on both sides of the mountains. Their hunting trail crossed what is now Yellowstone National Park and forded the Yellowstone River near Tower Fall.

Bannock Falls is a scenic off trail spot above Bradley Lake. The narrow chute of water, which is the first 100 feet, is only 4 feet wide. The stream then fans out over a series of steps to form the lower portion of the falls. Of the three falls on the stream from Middle Teton Glacier, Bannock Falls is the most difficult to reach and to photograph. The dense growth makes travel slow and photography tedious. An overcast day eliminates shadows produced by the many trees. An early morning outing might provide the best results.

HIKING TO BANNOCK FALLS: The strenuous hike to Bannock Falls begins at the Lupine Meadow Parking Area which is at the end of a spur road off Teton Park Road 7.5 miles north of

LOWER PORTION OF BANNOCK FALLS

Moose Junction and south of South Jenny Lake Junction. The small unpaved spur road leads 1.7 miles to the parking area.

Begin on the Amphitheater/Surprise Lake Trail to climb 700 feet in the first 1.7 miles to a trail junction. Continue on straight past the Valley Trail to climb to the third switchback. Leave the trail at the third switchback to travel down and to the south toward the creek.

Again, remember that all off trail hiking requires registration at the Jenny Lake Ranger Station. This precaution is for the safety of the hiker. The journey through the open meadow is easy and pleasant. However, the undergrowth is often thick as the forest gets more dense. It is easier to reach the stream lower than is necessary then travel upstream to Bannock Falls. (The beginning of this hike is the same as the beginning of the hike to Spalding and Cleft Falls.)

Another route is to take the Valley Trail over the first ridge and then venture off trail in a southwesterly direction to reach the stream below the falls. Still another possibility is to follow the stream up from Bradley Lake. This third option requires much bushwhacking and is the most difficult of the three.

Charles Maynard

SHOSHOKO FALLS

⫸ SHOSHOKO FALLS
100+ Feet

Roadside or 5 Mile Roundtrip - Shoshoko Falls can be viewed from the Teton Park Road or various vantage points on the Bradley -Taggart Lakes Loop Trail.

Shoshoko Falls is a double falls high in the Tetons in Avalanche Canyon. Mount Wister (11,490 feet) to the south and Nez Perce (11,901 feet) and Shadow Peak to the north frame Shoshoko Falls with snow-covered peaks. Shoshoko is a Shoshone word for "walker" meaning one who has no horse. A close-up visit to Shoshoko requires a long steep walk up Avalanche Canyon.

Shoshoko Falls can easily be viewed from afar. The North Fork of Taggart Creek, which cascades over the cliffs of Avalanche Canyon at 9,360 feet, is mostly snow melt. The water comes from the high Tetons near The Wall into Snowdrift Lake and Lake Taminah. Taminah is the Shoshone word for Spring. Due to its high elevation, Taminah is still spring-like well into summer, with patches of snow and spring wildflowers. Shoshoko shares the same fault line which partially causes Cleft Falls in Garnet Canyon and Hidden Falls at the mouth of Cascade Canyon.

Clumps of subalpine fir near the tree line dot the rocky cliffs about Shoshoko Falls. The stream drops in two separate side-by-side falls. The southerly (left) falls is very small for half its height where it strikes a ledge to spread into a beautiful silver fan. The northern (right) falls has a different character from its fraternal twin. The water falls in two small columns one fourth of the way down to hit a ledge where the two small falls unite in a large free fall to a rocky base.

The two falls mingle in the boulders which water and ice have dislodged from the cliff. A large cascade from the united stream can be seen downstream from the two upper falls.

Binoculars or a telephoto lens can bring this distant wonder closer. The falls can be enjoyed from the Taggart - Bradley Lakes Trail which is 2.5 miles from the falls.

HIKING TO A VIEW OF SHOSHOKO FALLS: Begin at the Taggart Lake Parking Area which is 3.5 miles north of Moose Junction on Teton Park Road. The hike starts in the open area which was cleared by the Beaver Creek Fire of 1985. The trail follows Taggart Creek up the moraine past several scenic small cascades.

At the trail junction the right branch goes to Bradley Lake which is in a green forested area. The trail to the left goes to Taggart Lake through an open area of dead trees left by a 1985 fire. Either trail will offer views of Shoshoko Falls high in Avalanche Canyon to the west.

It is possible to reach the base of Shoshoko Falls, but very difficult. All off trail hiking requires registration at a ranger station. Some basic mountain climbing skills are needed to make this trek. Shoshoko Falls can be viewed and enjoyed from afar.

THE TETONS FROM SNAKE RIVER OVERLOOK

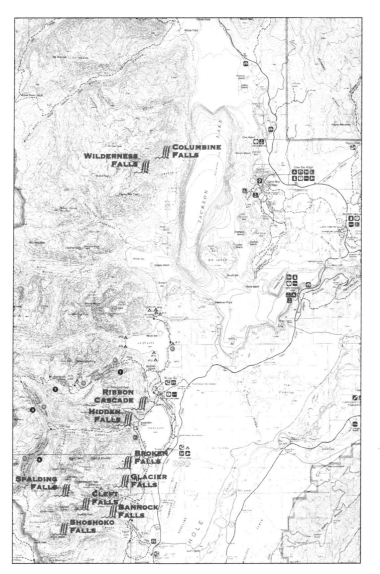

WILDERNESS FALLS

COLUMBINE FALLS

RIBBON CASCADE

HIDDEN FALLS

BROKEN FALLS

GLACIER FALLS

SPALDING FALLS

CLEFT FALLS

BANNOCK FALLS

SHOSHOKO FALLS

55

APPENDIX

WATERFALLS

Broken Falls	300+ feet
Wilderness Falls	250+ feet
Columbine Falls	200+ feet
Bannock Falls	200+ feet
Hidden Falls	200 feet
Shoshoko Falls	100+ feet
Ribbon Cascade	100+ feet
Spalding Falls	100+ feet
Glacier Falls	50 feet
Cleft Falls	50 feet

ROADSIDE

Wilderness Falls
Columbine Falls
Ribbon Cascade
Broken Falls
Glacier Falls
Shoshoko Falls

SHORT HIKES *1 to 5 Miles*

Hidden Falls	1.2 Miles
Hidden Falls	5.2 Miles
Shoshoko Falls	5.0 Miles

DAY HIKES *6 to 14 Miles*

Spalding Falls	10 Miles
Cleft Falls	8 Miles
Bannock Falls	6 Miles

Index

Bold type denotes photograph.

Maps

BIBLIOGRAPHY

Alt, David D. and Hyndman, David W. Roadside Geology of the Northern Rockies. Missoula, MT: Mountain Press Publishing Company, 1972.

Betts, Robert B. Along the Ramparts of the Tetons The Saga of Jackson Hole, Wyoming. Boulder, Colorado: Colorado Associated University Press, 1978.

Carter, Tom. Day Hiking Grand Teton National Park. Garland, Texas: Day Hiking Press, 1993.

Clark, Ella E. Indian Legends From The Northern Rockies. University of Oklahoma, 1966.

Grand Teton, A Guide to Grand Teton National Park. Washington, D. C.: Division of Publications National Park Service, 1984.

Harry, Bryan. Teton Trails. Moose, WY: Grand Teton Natural History Association, 1987.

Hayden, Elizabeth Wied and Nielsen, Cynthia. Origins, A Guide to the Place Names of Grand Teton National Park and the Surrounding Area. Moose, WY: Grand Teton Natural History Association, 1988.

Lawrence, Paul. Hiking the Teton Backcountry. San Francisco: Sierra Club Books, 1979.

Love, J.D. and Reed, John C., Jr. Creation of the Teton Landscape. Moose, WY: Grand Teton Natural History Association, 1989.

Olsen, Linda L. and Bywater, Tim. A Guide to Exploring Grand Teton National Park. Salt lake City, Utah: RMN Press, 1991.

Sanborn, Margaret. The Grand Tetons The Story of the Men Who Tamed the Western Wilderness. New York: G.P. Putnams's Sons, 1978.

Trails Illustrated Map of Grand Teton National Park, 1994.

ACKNOWLEDGEMENTS

Every book is the product of many people. I am truly grateful to the many who assisted and encouraged me on this project. This book would not have happened without Janice, my lifelong friend and wife. Her photographs, editing, encouragement, and love made it possible. Our daughters, Caroline and Anna, hiked to many waterfalls after riding all the way across the country. They encouraged, inspired and enlightened me while in the field and at home at the computer. I hope their memories of our adventurous summer will be as pleasant and cherished as my own.

True friends encourage dreams into reality. David Morris hiked to the toughest places to get the best photographs. His comments on the manuscript were always on target. I appreciate his wife, Lin and their sons, Ben and John, for loaning him to me for two weeks. Also, David's son, Brian, walked to the hardest and highest spots to help however needed. Brian's spirit brightened each long day on the trail. In working on this book Brian moved from being my friend's son to a true friend.

Other friends that stood by us in transition and in wild pursuits are Tom & Nancy Best, Hal & Elizabeth Hubbs, and Dan & Lynn Alexander. We literally couldn't have done it without them.

The staff of Grand Teton National Park was helpful and courteous. Patience in the face of many questions and requests is certainly a virtue. The park's library and photo collection was made available to me on several occasions.

I'm particularly indebted to my extended family and the people of St. Matthew United Methodist Church of Kingsport, Tennessee for their understanding and support as I pursued a dream.

About the Photographers

David Morris has long enjoyed hiking and backpacking and has visited several national parks. The combination of his love for the backcountry and his photographic skills allow him to capture images of the more remote subjects. He has several photographs published in books and magazines. Living in the foothills of the Smokies in Tennessee, he spend much of his free time as a volunteer in Great Smoky Mountains National Park. An active member of Souther Appalachian Nature Photographers, he continues the search for the perfect waterfall picture.

Janice Maynard is a teacher, author, and photographer. Her articles and picture have appeared in books, magazines, and newspapers. When she is not busy teaching second grade, she loves to travel an is an avid reader.

About the Author

*Charles Maynard is familiar with national parks throughout the United States. Having traveled extensively, Charles has written and edited numerous articles and books on national parks and waterfalls. As a columnist for **Yellowstone Journal** and a writer of **Waterfalls of Yellowstone National Park**, he is able to combine his love of the Rocky Mountains and waterfalls. Charles' affinity for national parks is displayed in his job as Executive Director of Friends of Great Smoky Mountains National Park. His wife, Janice, and their daughters, Caroline and Anna, assisted in the field work for this guide. The Maynards reside in Tennessee where they continue to write about and photograph waterfalls.*

Notes

Notes

Notes